How many parents a
hopes have been shat
prodigal children? What promises are available for
these parents to hold onto as they believe God for
the restoration of their beloved children? Lori
Wilkerson Stewart has put together the promises
that could be an anchor and blessing for those
Christian parents who are looking for answers in
God's word.

Pat Robertson
Chairman/Founder
The Christian Broadcasting Network, Inc.

For years I have witnessed so many prodigals that
have come to the end of the road of their wayward
journey from family and faith. I know the impact of
this on parents. Lori Wilkerson Stewart has given
parents and families a great resource of prayers
and Bible promises to give hope of the prodigal's
homecoming. I highly recommend this book!

Don Wilkerson
Co-Founder, Teen Challenge

When our loved ones wander from the heart of the
Father, the most powerful thing we can do on their
behalf is to pray. *Promises for Prodigals* sets a
biblical path before us to participate in our loved
one's journey of redemption. I encourage you to
make this book your own: write the name of your
"prodigal" in these prayers and scriptures and
commit the next 100 days to praying these
promises over his life—again and again!

Dr. Dick Eastman
International President, Every Home for Christ
President, America's National Prayer Committee

Anyone who has ever been a parent knows that children will increase your prayer life. At long last, you now have a guide. Lori Wilkerson Stewart has written a masterful compilation of promises to pray over your children and bring the promises of God to life in their lives. This book was born out of Lori's travail for her own child and it will birth in you the security of knowing that God watches over His word to perform it. Get it, pray it, and then live it.

Gordon Robertson
CEO, The Christian Broadcasting Network

If you, like me, have been the parent of a prodigal son or daughter, this book is for you! The Word of God moves mountains, strengthens us for the assignment before us, and brings peace in the storm. Take this to your prayer closet daily as you contend for your children. God is faithful to His promises. Our job is to declare them like a banner over each lost child. This book is a treasure to that end!

Terry Meeuwsen
Co-host, *The 700 Club*
Founder, Orphan's Promise

Promises for Prodigals is an incredible resource to pray over those we love who do not know Jesus. There is real peace and power to be found in the promises of God. As you declare the one hundred promises and prayers, I believe your heart will be lifted. This book will deeply encourage you.

Rich Wilkerson Jr.
Sr. Pastor, Vous Church
Author, *Sandcastle Kings* and *Friend of Sinners*

As Lori's older brother, I have watched her pursue her faith like few people I have ever met. Her ministry is known by many, but her desire to see lost children come back home to Jesus is unparalleled. In *Promises for Prodigals* you will be given a sure biblical plan to read and confess the Word over your loved one and pray the scripture perhaps like you never have before. Thank you Lori for never giving up!

Rich Wilkerson
Founder, Peacemakers International
Sr. Pastor, Trinity Church Miami/Harlem/San Diego

Promises for Prodigals

One Hundred Biblical Promises to
Declare Over Your Prodigal *Girl*

Lori Wilkerson Stewart

ISBN 978-1-71-779454-3

I dedicate this book to my #1 son, to my husband, Matt, and to my mother, Bonnie Wilkerson.
One inspired me to write the book, one loved me through the process, and one taught me how to trust in God's promises.

There's no shadow You won't light up
Mountain You won't climb up
Coming after me
There's no wall You won't kick down
Lie You won't tear down
Coming after me
O, the overwhelming, never-ending,
reckless love of God
O, it chases me down, fights 'til I'm
found, leaves the ninety-nine
I couldn't earn it, and I don't deserve
it, still You give Yourself away
O, the overwhelming, never-ending,
reckless love of God [1]

Introduction

On January 1 of 2011, the Lord gave me an unusual scripture, "But the Lord is with me like a *violent* warrior," Jeremiah 20:11. As I read it, I knew instantly that I was going to fight a difficult battle that year.

In March, we got a phone call from a trusted relative alerting us to some things going on in our oldest son's life. Without going into detail, he was living in sin. Our family confronted him; we said and did everything we could to change his mind, yet he remained determined to go down that path. What happened to the son who had given me 17 years of bliss? My perfect world was shattered. A few months later, my firstborn son graduated from high school and left home, moving 3,000 miles away. Nothing has been the same since.

I did the only thing I could do—pray and stand on God's word. Scripture after scripture gave me hope. I underlined them, prayed them, and copied them into journals. The Word truly became my weapon, and I wielded my sword against the enemy with more expertise each day.

Several years into this journey, I decided to make a book for my son. Each day,

I wrote down a scripture which I called his "promise," and I added a prayer to it. When I reached 100 promises, the book was full.

Now, I pray one of those 100 promises every day. This practice has given me incredible peace and purpose. *The word of God will not return void. It will accomplish what it is set forth to do* (Isaiah 55:11).

My son and I have a wonderful relationship in spite of our core values being wildly different. I love him fiercely and he knows it. One day he will also realize how passionately he is loved by his Heavenly Father. Until that day, I will continue to pray and believe that my prodigal will come home.

If this book has found its way into your hands, it is no accident. As you pray these promises, believe and know that God is setting your prodigal free. I have left blanks in the prayers for you to write in the name of your loved one. In the original book for my son, I also took the liberty of adding his name to some of the Bible verses, and I encourage you to do the same—that is why some of the verses also have a blank. I did that in place of words like *Israel*—the general idea is that whether a group of people or one person wanders from God, it is God's will that we come back to the Father. In addition, I changed some of the "he" pronouns in the Bible verses to "she" pronouns. In those cases, "she" is in italics.

I made a girl version of the original book for a few reasons. First, my parents, family members, countless friends and I prayed for decades for my older sister to come back to Jesus. God heard and answered our prayers! My sister accepted Christ in her 40's and is serving and loving God wholeheartedly to this day. Second, when I read other books written for parents with prodigals, I found that pronouns matter. I wanted your prayer journey for your loved one to be as personal as possible.

Finally, I wrote the following verses at the back of my original promise book to encourage me. I urge you to keep them in mind as you pray, especially during times when it seems nothing is happening:

Each promise is backed by the honor of His name (Ps. 138:2b).

ALL the Lord's promises prove true (Ps. 18:30).

Day 1 Promise

But the love of the Lord remains forever with those who fear him. His salvation extends to the children's children.

Psalm 103:17

My Prayer

Because I fear the Lord and because I have received salvation, my child is promised salvation. It is her birthright! _Hailey_, this great salvation is yours for the asking. Jesus, this promise says your love is eternally with my family. Reveal your love to _Hailey_ today!

Lord, wherever she is and whatever she is doing, please remind her who she is: a daughter of the most high God. Help her remember her childhood fondly. How she loved going to church, singing songs to you, hearing stories about you, and being around your people. May she yearn for the God of her childhood.

Today I declare the promise to the children's children: ~~one day~~ _Hailey_ ~~will be~~ _is_ saved!

Day 2 Promise

Now all glory to God, who is able to keep you from falling away and will bring you with great joy into his glorious presence without a single fault.

Jude 1:24

My Prayer

Lord, this promise puts me in a mood to praise you! One day _____ will choose to surrender her life to you. She will break free of her chains and will serve you faithfully until that final day.

I see her entering your throne room... not with her head down in shame, but with her eyes bright, looking at the One she adores. She will not be found guilty of a single thing. Right now she is drowning in muck and mire; but on that day she walks tall, eager to receive her rewards as a rightful heir. Please give her a divine glimpse into her future. I ask that even now she experiences your glorious presence.

Today I declare that someday Jesus will present _____ to the Father with great joy. Heaven will celebrate!

Day 3 Promise

Our children will also serve him.

Psalm 22:30a

My Prayer

Father, I am your faithful follower. Serving you has been my greatest joy and delight. Knowing you gives my life significance and meaning. I want the same for _____. She is floundering out there; a young woman full of gifts, talents, and abilities, but sin robs her of any real purpose in life.

This verse promises that my future seed, my tribe, my posterity is destined to serve you. I believe in generational blessings! Your word says you maintain loving devotion for a thousand generations to those who love and obey you (Deut. 7:9). How great is your faithfulness!

Today I declare that one day _____ will also serve you!

Day 4 Promise

He has promised that you will escape the
decadence all around you caused by evil
desires and that you will share in his divine
nature.

2 Peter 1:4

My Prayer

Lord, I thank you for already providing
a way of escape for _____. I believe this
promise—one day she will want out! Right
now she cannot imagine her life without the
sin she craves. I pray it begins to make her
sick—that she becomes physically disgusted
with worldly pleasures. In Jesus name, I break
a spirit of lust, and I pray you will replace it
with real love.

Jesus, only you can change the way
people think, the things they desire. I pray
_____ experiences true, godly repentance.
Do a deep inner work in her heart and mind.
You do not save people half-way. You save to
the uttermost!

Today I declare that one day _____
will escape the world's corruption and take on
the very nature of Christ!

Day 5 Promise

You have been taught the Holy Scriptures from childhood, and they have given you the wisdom to receive the salvation that comes by trusting in Christ Jesus.

2 Timothy 3:15

My Prayer

Dear God, you know I did my best to teach my beloved your word. She has heard countless Bible teachings and memorized dozens of key scriptures. And when I think of all the Christian songs she once loved—too many to count! I believe your word is a seed planted deep in her heart, and one day it will bear fruit.

Paul told Timothy to remain faithful to the things he had been taught. Paul added, "You can trust those who taught you"(2 Tim. 3:14). Right now, would you remind _____of all the saints who taught her? As she reflects on all the trustworthy men and women who poured into her, she will know every scripture, every story, every song was true.

Today I declare that _____ has the wisdom to receive salvation and one day she will trust Jesus with her life!

Day 6 Promise

He fulfills the desires of those who fear him;
he hears their cries for help and rescues them.

Psalm 145:19

My Prayer

Lord, my greatest desire is to see all my
children loving and serving you. My heart
longs to see _____ at ease around us, with
nothing to prove, no agenda, no angle, walls
down, laughing and goofing around with the
family. Once again sharing our values, our
core beliefs, and our love for Jesus.

The day is coming when she will wake
up and realize the danger she is in, and when
that day comes will you remind her of the
power of your name? Just one word is all it
takes: "Jesus."

Today I declare this promise: when
_____ cries for help, you will rescue her!

Day 7 Promise

He lifted _____ up and carried _____
through all the years.

Isaiah 63:9b

My Prayer

Lord, even your word acknowledges that
sin is fun for a season. But that season has
passed. She has grown tired and weary of her
empty, pleasure-seeking life. It is time for her
to surrender. I love this verse—I see a tired
young girl reaching up for help, and her daddy
scooping her up and carrying her in his big,
strong arms. I praise you Father, for I know
that is what you are doing for _____.

Today I declare that Jesus—*right now*—
is carrying _____ to safety!

There is no problem too big God cannot solve it
There is no mountain too tall He cannot move it
There is no storm too dark God cannot calm it
There is no sorrow too deep He cannot soothe it
Oh, if He carried the weight of the world upon His
shoulders
Oh, I know my sister that He will carry you [2]

Day 8 Promise

"... I would not forget you. See, I have written your name on my hand." -the Lord

Isaiah 49:15b-16a

My Prayer

Just as a loving mother cannot forget her child, it is not possible for you to forget _____. Lord, you have gone to extreme lengths to remember her—even tattooing her name on your hand! Each time you think of _____, will you give her a God wink? Show her something that will remind her of your goodness and compassion. Put kind, caring Christians in her path. Prompt them to share words of wisdom and knowledge with her.

Today I declare that _____ will know that you are thinking about her!

Day 9 Promise

Those who plant in tears will harvest with shouts of joy.

Psalm 126:5

My Prayer

Lord, only you know how many tears I have cried for _____. You understand that each one is precious and costly. I praise you that not one was shed in vain!

Each tear is like a seed, planted in the ground, hidden away. There are days when I cannot see anything happening, but I know that in due season, that seed will burst forth with life! I am so thankful that all my weeping will not be wasted.

Today I declare this promise: one day a great harvest of joy is coming! What once appeared dead has come back to life! The prodigal daughter is home!

Day 10 Promise

"Anything is possible if a person believes."
-Jesus
Mark 9:23

My Prayer

Lord, I believe you will set _____ free, because you came to set the captive free. You also came to give us life more abundantly. Jesus, you do not just save us *from* something, but you save us *for* something.

One day a father brought his son who was tormented by an impure spirit to you. He asked you to heal him and you spoke these powerful words to him: *Anything is possible.* He replied, "Lord, I believe! Help me overcome my unbelief" (Mark 9:24)! Just like that father, I bring _____ to you, and I ask you to set her free from impure spirits. Fill me with faith and remove any unbelief.

Today I declare freedom and total breakthrough for _____! I believe she will live a victorious life in Christ Jesus!

There is nothing impossible with God. All the impossibility is with us when we measure God by the limitations of our unbelief.[3]
Smith Wigglesworth

Day 11 Promise

"For I know the plans I have for you," declares the Lord, "plans to prosper you and not to harm you, plans to give you a hope and a future."

Jeremiah 29:11

My Prayer

Lord, your plans for _____ are beyond all I could ever hope or imagine, and I can think up some pretty incredible scenarios! Thank you for including the "not to harm you" part, because sometimes I worry that with each bad decision she is asking for the wrath of God to fall upon her. But you are not like that! You are not keeping score or looking for any excuse to punish her. In fact, your mercy always triumphs over judgment.

I love how this verse ends with the best promise of all: *a hope and a future*. Wow! Your plans extend far beyond this life. They are eternal purposes. Today I declare that one day _____ will choose your plan! May she live out her eternal purpose with hope and prosperity!

Day 12 Promise

When _____ prays to the Lord,
_____ will be accepted. And God will
receive *her* with joy and restore *her* to good
standing.

Job 33:26

My Prayer

Lord, this verse captures your character
so beautifully—you receive and you restore.
The question I am asking is, "When?" Your
answer, "When *she* prays." She certainly
knows how…

I remember when she was a little girl,
each night she would say her prayers before
going to bed. Praying was effortless and each
one was loaded with childlike faith. Now she
seems so far from you, but the truth is … she
is only one prayer away. One prayer. That is
all.

I pray that divine circumstances will
prompt her to pray. Whether her prayer is a
whisper, a shout, a cry, or a whimper, I know
you will be waiting to accept her with open
arms.

Today I declare that _____ will
pray to the Lord, and God will welcome her
back with joy!

Day 13 Promise

The earnest prayer of a righteous person has great power and wonderful results.

James 5:16

My Prayer

Lord, I thank you that I am made righteous because of the cleansing blood of Jesus. When I pray in your powerful name, I am guaranteed results. When I think of all the righteous people who partner with me in prayer for _____, I am humbled and my faith rises. God, thank you for each and every faithful intercessor.

Today I declare that our earnest prayers for _____ will achieve extraordinary results: salvation, deliverance, and abundant life!

We can change the course of events if we go to our knees in believing prayer.[4] Billy Graham

Day 14 Promise

Patient endurance is what you need now, so you will continue to do God's will. Then you will receive all that he has promised.

Hebrews 10:36

My Prayer

Lord, this verse reminds me that I am in a war, not a battle, and wars are not won overnight. I must confidently trust you, and no matter what happens, I will not give up. I believe one day I will live to see all God's promises for _____ come to pass!

As I wait for the fulfillment of the promises, help me to do your will. Keep me from bitterness and offense, because sometimes my flesh wants to blame you for her problems. How foolish of me to turn against you, when you are my greatest hope! Help me to keep an attitude of praise, especially when I receive bad news.

Today I declare that God has fortified me with patient endurance to do God's will! I will keep praying and claiming all God's promises for _____!

Day 15 Promise

They will not conquer _____, for I will
protect and deliver _____. I, the Lord,
have spoken!

Jeremiah 15:20b

My Prayer

Lord, your beloved girl is surrounded by
enemies on all sides. Each day they try to take
another piece of her. You and I know she was
born to influence others, but instead they are
influencing her for evil. That is why I thank
you for this promise: _____ will NOT be
defeated! Even though all appears lost, you
are going to bring deliverance! This promise is
sealed with the sound of your voice, so full of
power and authority. Who would dare to defy
the spoken word of the Almighty God? No one!
Today I declare that the enemy will not
conquer _____. Even now, the Lord is
personally protecting her and delivering her.

Day 16 Promise

Look and see, for all your children will come back to you... they will be like jewels or bridal ornaments for you to display.

Isaiah 49:18

My Prayer

Lord, give me eyes to see and a heart to believe that the day is coming when _____ will come back to our family. She will be like a priceless jewel to display—what a proud moment for me! I will show her off to everyone!

Help me to live with expectancy! After all, it could be today! Any minute now the phone could ring, she could knock on the front door, or maybe I will get a text. Lord, I am looking and I am eagerly awaiting her return. I know that faith is what pleases you, so I will keep the faith.

Today I declare that _____ will come back to us! It will be this family's proudest moment. We will show the world what our great God has done!

Day 17 Promise

I pray that your heart will be flooded with light so that you can understand the wonderful future he has promised to those he called.

Ephesians 1:18a

My Prayer

Thank you Lord, that as I pray you are drawing _____ out of darkness and flooding the atmosphere around her with light. This prayer comes with a promise: when the light comes, so does understanding. Give her a waking vision of the wonderful future that awaits her the moment she surrenders her life to you. I pray it will be so real to her that she cannot deny it. Let her grasp the glorious inheritance that is her birthright—a wonderful, rich, beautiful life in Christ.

Today I declare that _____ will see the light! Let her desire this wonderful future you have promised her!

Day 18 Promise

"It is not my heavenly Father's will that even one of these little ones should perish." -Jesus

Matthew 18:14

My Prayer

Jesus, you are the Good Shepherd. You leave the ninety-nine sheep to go after the little lamb who wanders away and gets lost. I thank you that even now you are pursuing _____. It is the Father's will that you find her and bring her back to the fold. Not only that, but when you bring the lost one home, you will rejoice over her more than the others who did not wander away. Such mercy! Such love!

Today, I declare the Father's will for _____. She will not perish, but she will be found. The Good Shepherd will bring her home, and we will all rejoice!

Day 19 Promise

"Humanly speaking, it is impossible. But with God, everything is possible." –Jesus

Matthew 19:26

My Prayer

Lord, I confess sometimes I look at my prodigal from a purely human perspective. When I do, her situation starts to look hopeless. When the disciples asked you who could be saved, you acknowledged this. But you did not stop there. You turned their gaze up—"But with God…"

I thank you for reminding me that I am in a spiritual battle. It will not be won with human wit, ideas, strategies, or manipulation. This is God's fight! And with God, everything is possible!

Today I declare that with God's help, _____ will be saved! There is absolutely nothing my God cannot do!

Day 20 Promise

The unfailing love of the Lord never ends! By his mercies we have been kept from complete destruction.

Lamentations 3:22

My Prayer

Lord, I thank you for your unfailing love and mercy for _____. She is walking through a mine field, and you have kept her from being destroyed. Make her aware of the daily mercies you show her—that they are not chance or coincidence, but the Holy Spirit trying to get her attention! May she know in her heart you are performing acts of love specifically aimed at her.

Today I declare that one day _____ will praise you for your faithful, unfailing love that rescued her from imminent destruction. She will tell others of your endless mercy and help lead many to safety!

Day 21 Promise

Then they will come to their senses and escape from the devil's trap. For they have been held captive by him...

II Timothy 2:26

My Prayer

In Jesus name, wake up and remember who you are _____! You are part of a royal priesthood, God's special possession, a citizen of heaven. You were born to praise the great I AM!

Lord, she is so confused. I ask that you send people to gently teach her the truth. Give her a sound mind, so she can discern truth from lies. God, only you can change her heart and help her believe again.

Today I declare that _____ will come to her senses and escape from captivity! No longer a slave in service to the devil, but a daughter, an heir, a child of the Most High God. Freedom is here!

Day 22 Promise

He lives forever to plead with God on
_____'s behalf.

Hebrews 7:25b

My Prayer

Jesus, I thank you that you are
constantly interceding to the Father for
_____. What a powerful advocate she has!
Sometimes people tell me they are praying for
our family, and maybe they do and maybe they
don't. Not true with you! How wonderful that
even while I am sleeping, or working, or just
going about my day, you never stop praying
for my prodigal. Hallelujah!

Today I declare this promise: _____
has a High Priest that pleads with God on her
behalf!

Come running, come running, come running to the
mercy seat
Where Jesus is calling, His grace will be your
covering.
His blood will flow freely,
It will provide your healing.
Come running to the mercy seat.[5]

Day 23 Promise

And we will receive whatever we request because we obey him and do the things that please him.

I John 3:22

My Prayer

Lord, this promise is gold and I can bank on it. So I come boldly to your throne and ask that you save _____. I know you will!

In the meantime, help me to walk in obedience and faith. Your word says that faith is what pleases you. Sometimes my faith is so strong, and I experience peace that passes understanding. I love days like that. Other times, out of nowhere, I get some information that takes my breath away and knocks my legs out from under me. In those times, help me to hold up the shield of faith and pick up my sword—all these powerful promises—to fight for my beloved!

Today I declare that I will receive my request! _____ will give her life to you and fulfill her God-given destiny!

Day 24 Promise

"I have made _____ for myself, and
_____ will someday honor me before
the whole world."   -the Lord

Isaiah 43:21

My Prayer

Lord, _____ is fearfully and
wonderfully made—full of gifts, talents, and
abilities that make her so unique. She is
created in your image. She carries your DNA.
What a one-of-a-kind treasure! What a
priceless masterpiece!

The enemy knows this. That is why he
stole your treasure. Jesus, you knew
_____ would need rescuing. You have
already paid her ransom with your shed blood.
You are her Redeemer, and you love her.

Today, I declare that _____ belongs
to you, Jesus, and one day she will help make
your name famous in all the earth!

Day 25 Promise

God wants _____ to be saved and to understand the truth.

I Timothy 2:4

My Prayer

Jesus, you are "the way, the truth, and the life" (John 14:6). My beloved is searching for truth. She was taught the truth as a girl, but there must have been some disconnect, some misunderstanding. Holy Spirit, I ask you to help her comprehend and grasp all that she already knows. Jesus, will you reveal yourself to _____? Will you show her that ALL truth is found in you?

God, you clearly want everyone to be saved. You gave us your only Son to make that possible. You also gave us a free will, so please do whatever it takes to turn her heart toward you.

Today I declare God's will and desire for _____: salvation and truth!

Day 26 Promise

Believe on the Lord Jesus and you will be
saved, along with your entire household.
Acts 16:31

My Prayer

Joshua said, "As for me and my house,
we will serve the Lord"(Joshua 25:15b). Our
family made that same decision a long time
ago. You are a God who cares about the family
unit. That's why we still call you the God of
Abraham, Isaac, and Jacob.

Lord, I claim this promise for my
family. Because I believe in the Lord Jesus, I
declare that one day our entire household will
be saved.

*Our prayers are genesis moments that create and
change our genealogy.*[6] Mark Batterson

Day 27 Promise

And remember, the Lord is waiting so that
people have time to be saved.

II Peter 3:15a

My Prayer

Lord, thank you for waiting to return
until _____ is saved. Your patience, your
kindness, your gentleness, and your peace in
the process—all of these speak of your great
love.

Your Word says that you make *all*
things beautiful in your time (Eccl. 3:11). I
believe that you are devising divine events
that will one day culminate in her salvation.
Help me remember that these things take
time. Even when I cannot see progress, you
are working while I am waiting. The end of
this story will be breathtakingly beautiful. To
God be the glory!

Today I declare that _____ will not
wait too late, for you are the God of perfect
timing!

Day 28 Promise

I will be with _____ constantly until I
have finished giving _____ everything I
have promised.

Genesis 28:15

My Prayer

Lord, thank you for this assurance. You
are Jehovah Shammah- *the Lord is there.* You
will constantly be with _____ until all the
promises in this book are fulfilled. She is
never alone. Let her be aware of your presence
each day. Thank you for being her faithful
friend that sticks closer than a brother.

Today I declare the promise of your
presence. God is with _____ wherever she
goes.

Day 29 Promise

The Lord stands beside me like a violent warrior... they cannot defeat me.

Jeremiah 20:11a

My Prayer

Lord, I thank you for being right beside me as I battle in prayer for _____. The lion of the tribe of Judah fights with me. Talk about a fixed fight! The enemy flees in terror, utterly humiliated!

Help me keep my eyes on you when I get weary and start to lose faith. Give me fresh courage to fight on. Remind me that the battle is the Lord's.

Today I declare that God is fighting with me to free _____ from the enemy. Victory is inevitable!

Day 30 Promise

I will give _____ a new heart with new and right desires ... I will take out *her* stony heart of sin and give *her* a new, obedient heart.

Ezekiel 36:26

My Prayer

Lord, only you can give someone a new heart. Only you can change a person's desires. You and only you have the power to transform!

I ask you to give _____ a new heart and right desires. Let her heart become tender and obedient, wanting only those things that please you.

Today I declare total transformation for _____! People all over the world will see the change in her and give you ALL the glory!

Day 31 Promise

For God so loved the world that he gave his only Son, so that everyone who believes in him will not perish but have eternal life.

John 3:16

My Prayer

Lord, she knows this verse by heart, yet somehow she no longer believes. I pray _____ starts to see and hear this verse everywhere she goes. When she does, let her see the words with fresh eyes and hear them again for the first time. Holy Spirit, let the truth of this scripture resonate deep in her soul and awaken her spirit! You love _____ SO much you gave your only Son to die so that she can live. Give her the faith to believe and to trust you with her life.

Today I declare the John 3:16 promise for _____: believe in Jesus and receive everlasting life!

Day 32 Promise

God's Holy Spirit ... has identified _____
as his own, guaranteeing that _____ will
be saved.

Ephesians 4:30

My Prayer

Lord, you filled _____ with your
Holy Spirit when she accepted Jesus as a
child. In that moment, you guaranteed that on
the day of redemption, she will be saved.

She struggles with her identity, Lord. It
breaks my heart to see what lengths she goes
to looking for acceptance and a place to
belong. Deliver her from the way she lives; I
know it grieves you, Holy Spirit. Lead her to
repentance and restore her. Help her realize
her true identity can only be found in Christ.
Give _____ a revelation of who she is: a
beloved child of God!

Today I declare that the Holy Spirit has
marked _____ as his own, guaranteeing
salvation. Hallelujah! God always keeps his
promises!

Day 33 Promise

I will be your God throughout your lifetime—
until your hair is white with age. I made you,
and I will care for you. I will carry you along
and save you. Isaiah 46:4

My Prayer

I love this lifetime promise! Lord, you
knew _____ even before she was born.
She was dedicated to you as a baby, loved and
cared for throughout her childhood and
beyond. Somewhere along the way, we started
to lose her—it seemed surreal. Was this really
happening to us? Then, all too soon, she was
gone. Through all the soul searching,
questions, and tears, you have been faithful. It
brings me endless comfort to know she is not
alone. Even when she wants nothing to do
with you, you are right there by her side.

Father, she desperately needs your
loving care now. She has fallen so far down;
will you pick her up and carry her to safety? I
know you will, because you never go back on
your word.

Today I declare that _____ belongs
to God; she always has and she always will.
You created her, you care for her and you will
save her!

Day 34 Promise

Therefore he is able, once and forever, to save everyone who comes to God through Him.

Hebrews 7:25a

My Prayer

Lord, when this is over it will be as though _____ never even sinned. You don't save a person halfway, you save completely. You make our sins—which are red as crimson—white as wool. No stains left whatsoever. Praise God!

Your word says that no one comes to the Father unless the Holy Spirit draws them (John 6:44). Holy Spirit, I ask you to pursue _____ and turn her heart toward her Heavenly Father.

Today I declare a once-and-for-all salvation for _____. The old is gone and the new is come! Let her life proclaim, *I have decided to follow Jesus. No turning back, no turning back!* [7]

Day 35 Promise

The Lord called me before my birth; from within the womb He called me by name … He said to me, "You are my servant, _____, and you will bring me glory."

Isaiah 49:1b, 3

My Prayer

Lord, you called _____ and chose her before she was born to bring you glory. I am ready to see this promise fulfilled. It will be miraculous and beautiful to behold!

I pray you will put a sense of destiny in her. Make her aware that she is way off the mark now, that this is not the life you intended for her. You have so much more for her! _____ was born to serve you, enjoy you, and worship you—and one day she will!

Today I declare that _____ will hear you call her name, and she will say "Yes" to the call of God on her life. She will live to serve you and bring you glory!

Day 36 Promise

"So if the Son sets you free, you will be
free indeed." - Jesus

John 8:36

My Prayer

Jesus, you taught that sin and slavery
go hand-in-hand. My prodigal thinks she is
making her own choices, but in reality she is a
slave to sin. Sin is her diabolical master,
controlling everything she does.

Lord, you are the Way, the Truth and
the Life. You said that when we know the
Truth, the Truth will set us free.

Today I declare freedom from sin for
_____! Let her know you, the Truth, and
make her truly free!

Day 37 Promise

For God is working in _____, giving
_____ the desire to obey him and the
power to do what pleases him.

Philippians 2:13

My Prayer

Father, none of us can live this
Christian life in our own strength. Show
_____ that you can change her desires.
Holy Spirit, you will provide the power she
needs to live a righteous life.

Jesus, so much of her faith struggle
comes down to surrendering control. Will you
please help her let go? Teach her to trust you
and submit to your will.

Today I declare that the Holy Spirit is
working in _____, changing her desires
and giving her the power to live for God.

Day 38 Promise

But whenever anyone turns to the Lord, then
the veil is taken away.

2 Corinthians 3:16

My Prayer

Lord, remove the veil covering her eyes
and mind that keep her from seeing and
understanding the truth.

In Jesus name, turn to the Lord,
_____! Open your eyes and look upon the
One who loves you! The One who is able to set
you free! The glory of God lives inside you.
Stop hiding. Stop covering up the real you.
Take off the veil and let the light within you
shine for all to see!

Today I declare that _____ will
turn to the Lord! She will be like a mirror that
brightly reflects God's glory!

Day 39 Promise

So, dear _____, you have no obligation whatsoever to do what your sinful nature urges you to do... But if through the power of the Holy Spirit you turn from it and its evil deeds, you will live.

Romans 8:12, 13b

My Prayer

Thank you, Lord, for the life-giving power of the Holy Spirit that is able to free us from the power of sin.

Holy Spirit, I pray that _____ turns to you for the power she needs to overcome her sinful nature. Put a godly fear in her that if she continues on this path she will perish. That is the harsh reality, and I want her to face the truth. I also know it is your kindness that draws us to repentance, so give her a sneak peak at what her life can be if she surrenders to you! You are a good father, and you have good things in store for your children.

Today I believe and declare that _____ will live free from sinful urges and evil deeds! She will live as God's beloved child, adopted into his family, a co-heir with Christ!

Day 40 Promise

The godly walk with integrity; blessed are
their children after them.

Proverbs 20:7

My Prayer

Father, you are the God who "lavishes
love for a thousand generations" to those who
follow and obey you (Ex. 20:6). You keep your
covenant to the children's children, and with
that covenant comes blessing. This promise
means that _____ has favored status with
God and endowed power for success. To think
the Master and Creator of the universe is
chasing her down in hopes to give her a
blessing—I stand speechless, jaw-dropped, in
awe. Such radical love!

Today I declare God's covenant blessing
for _____. All praise and glory to the God
of infinite mercy and generous grace! Thank
you for undeserved blessings!

Day 41 Promise

And now, all glory to God, who is able to keep you from stumbling, and who will bring you into his glorious presence innocent of sin and with great joy.

Jude 1:24

My Prayer

Lord, I feel as if she accidentally stumbled into quicksand, foolishly missed her chance to get out, and now she is being buried alive. She sinks further down each day, while sin sucks the life out of her. Please rescue her and pull her to safety. I know you will. When she is rescued, there is always the fear that she could get sucked right back in—this promise assures me that *will not* happen.

Today I declare that you are the God with keeping power! All glory to the One who can save _____, keep her from falling, and present her innocent before the Father. I cannot wait for that day!

When we all get to heaven, what a day of rejoicing that will be!
When we all see Jesus, we'll sing and shout the victory! [8]

Day 42 Promise

And we can be confident that he will listen to us whenever we ask for anything in line with his will. And ... he will give us what we ask for.

I John 5:14, 15b

My Prayer

Jesus, this reminds me of the story you told about the woman who kept asking the unjust judge for help. Finally, he gave in—all because of her persistence! You also told of a man who repeatedly asked his neighbor for bread in the middle of the night, and the neighbor finally got up and gave him the bread. Lord, you clearly want me to keep asking, so I will.

Lord, I am confident that when I ask you to save my beloved, I am praying according to your will. So I will ask again: please save _____ and do it soon!

Today I declare that God hears my prayer to save _____. I am absolutely, positively sure he will give me what I am asking for!

Day 43 Promise

You listened to my pleading; you heard my weeping. Yes, *you came* at my despairing cry and told me, "Do not fear."

Lamentations 3:56, 57

My Prayer

Lord, I admit this promise is for me. Thank you for always hearing my cries for _____. I do not fear for the future, because I know you will answer my cry. Lord, save her!

Jeremiah prayed this prayer from deep inside a well. His enemies threw him down the well and even dropped stones on him! Drowning, Jeremiah thought his life was over. Then, *you came.*

Thank God my situation is not to this extreme! But sometimes I do feel like I am drowning in a pit of despair. While I am flailing around down there, the enemy throws his lies down on me, weighing me down even further. But that is not how the story ends...

Today I declare that when you hear my desperate cries you will come and lift me up. You will wrap me in a garment of praise and lift the spirit of heaviness right off of me!

Day 44 Promise

"But I have pleaded in prayer for you,
_____, that your faith should not fail. So
when you have repented and turned to me
again, strengthen and build up your brothers."

-Jesus

Luke 22:32

My Prayer

Dear Jesus, thank you for pleading for
_____ to keep the faith. I know dormant
seeds of faith are still alive in her. With the
right conditions, those seeds will germinate
and grow. Each seed was planted in good soil,
for she once loved you and received your word
with joy. Lord, I ask that you start activating
those seeds within her.

Jesus, I love that you have faith for
_____. You said, "*When* you have
repented and turned." Not *if,* but *when*!

How perfect that you include purpose in
this promise—you want her to "strengthen
and build up" others. Despite our past
mistakes, you do not disqualify us from
serving in your kingdom.

Today I declare that one day _____
will turn to Jesus. She will be a strong
witness and an encourager to others! Amen!

Day 45 Promise

Lord, you alone are my inheritance, my cup of blessing. You guard all that is mine.

Psalm 16:5

My Prayer

I thank you for your protection over my family, especially _____. You guard her "as the apple of your eye" (Ps. 17:6). You surround her with your "shield of love" (Ps. 5:12). Every promise prayed over her is her "armor and protection" (Ps. 91:4). The enemy cannot touch her without your permission— she is under the watchful care of the Lord's mighty army!

Today I declare God's promise to guard all that is mine; he is protecting _____ from physical harm. Praise Jehovah Nissi, *our great God is a banner of love and protection!*

Day 46 Promise

"And I will pour out my Spirit and my
blessings on your children. They will thrive ..."
-the Lord
Isaiah 44:3, 4a

My Prayer

Lord, let _____ thrive like a tree
growing next to a riverbank. I pray you pour
out your Holy Spirit on her, filling her with
power to overcome sin, to share your love, and
to create beauty. I believe others will see and
acknowledge how God is blessing her. When
they do, let her "proudly claim, *I belong to the
Lord"* (Is. 44:5).

Today I declare that one day
_____ will thrive! Fill her with your
Spirit and load her with daily blessings!

Day 47 Promise

I could have no greater joy than to hear that my children live in the truth.

III John 4

My Prayer

Lord, this is me! I believe "greater joy" is coming. I know that one day _____ will live in the truth.

Jesus, somewhere in her past the enemy planted lies in her mind. The lies took root and a lying spirit took up residence in her. I come against that demonic spirit in the NAME of JESUS, and I command it to *GO!* Holy Spirit, replace all those lies with your truth. May she live in the reality of God's love.

Today I declare that great joy is coming! The truth will set _____ free!

Day 48 Promise

Those who have been ransomed by the Lord
will return...they will be overcome with joy
and gladness.

Isaiah 35:10

My Prayer

Lord, you know my prodigal has been
kidnapped and held as a slave. Her captor,
Satan, didn't ask for money; he demanded the
life of your own Son. I thank you that
_____ is free to leave at any time,
because Jesus already paid the price for her
ransom when he willingly died on the cross.

_____, did you hear the good news?
Your ransom was paid and you are free to go!

Jesus, I believe when she really
comprehends what you have done for her,
_____ will be overcome with joy. I picture
her laughing, crying happy tears, dancing,
jumping, singing, shouting, and grinning ear-
to-ear!

Today I declare that _____ has
been ransomed by the Lord and she will gladly
return home!

Day 49 Promise

God is our refuge and strength, always ready
to help in times of trouble.

Psalm 46:1

My Prayer

Jesus, I love that you are *always ready*
to help your children. _____ is in
trouble, and she needs you desperately. The
problem is ... she still does not want to admit
it. Humble her, Lord. I pray she runs to you
for safety when she is in danger. Let her turn
to you when she feels weak and needs
strength.

Today I declare you are ready and able
to help _____ face all of life's challenges.
You are her eternal refuge and never-ending
source of strength!

Day 50 Promise

The children of your people will live in security. Their children's children will thrive in your presence.

Psalm 102:28

My Prayer

Lord, I pray that _____ will live in security. Please lead her to the right job and move her into a stable environment. Her living situation is anything but secure, and I ask you to open up a godly home where she can live and begin to thrive.

You also include a promise that future generations will live in your presence. I believe one day she will be a mother and/or a spiritual mother to many, and I pray those dear ones will come to know you and enjoy you forever!

Today I declare the promise of security for _____. Thank you for your gracious generosity to her!

Day 51 Promise

To discipline and reprimand a child produces
wisdom ...
Discipline your children, and they will give
you happiness and peace of mind.

Proverbs 29: 15, 17

My Prayer

Lord, I see a promise here for
_____ and for the people who raised her.
We made sure to consistently discipline her
with love. Godly correction comes with a
future guarantee: wisdom! Right now she is
not making the best decisions, but I believe
one day she will. There is wisdom in
_____; I pray she hears and obeys the
voice of wisdom guiding her, saying, "This is
the way; walk in it" (Isaiah 30:21).

God, I thank you for including us in this
promise. Because we faithfully corrected her
and taught her self-control throughout her
early years, I know one day _____ will
give us happiness and peace of mind.

Today I declare that _____ is a
woman of wisdom. As a woman filled with the
Holy Spirit and governed by self-discipline,
she will make right choices that bring joy to
others.

Day 52 Promise

And I am sure that God, who began the good work within _____, will continue his work until it is finally finished ...

Philippians 1:6

My Prayer

Lord, you have been with _____ from her first breath. The beginning of her journey was SO good, and I thank you for the sweet memories. When I think back, I see God's intentional goodness imparted to her during every stage of her life. I praise you that even now, your goodness is pursuing her.

God, you are a finisher! I am ready to see the *good work* continue in her life. Thank you for never giving up on my prodigal, Lord.

Today I declare that God will finish the good work he started in _____! On the day Christ returns, your work in her will be complete.

Day 53 Promise

"...I will pour out my Spirit upon all people...
Your sons and daughters will prophecy."

-the Lord
Joel 2:28

My Prayer

Lord, you promised that in the last days
your Holy Spirit would give our young women
a revelation of God's divine will. Throughout
your word, you revealed yourself through
prophetic words and visions to people who had
a difficult job to do. Those jobs required an
extra measure of faith. The young women of
this generation also have a tough assignment
—to prepare the way for your second coming.

Your word says that "where there is no
vision, the people perish" (Prov. 29:18). My
prodigal lacks clear vision and purpose; she
flounders about unrestrained. I am asking you
to give _____ a life-changing, eye-
opening, soul-revealing vision of Jesus.

Today I declare the promise that
_____ will receive prophetic words from
heaven as your Holy Spirit is poured out upon
her!

Day 54 Promise

"Oh _____, stay away from idols! I am
the one who looks after you and cares for you."

-the Lord
Hosea 14:8a

My Prayer

Lord, my prodigal no longer worships
you. Instead, she is obsessed with worldly
things—the lust of the flesh, the lust of the
eyes, and the pride of life (1 John 2:16).
Forgive her for putting possessions and selfish
desires ahead of her love for you. Turn her
attention to the one who loves and cares for
her: YOU! Jesus, you are worthy of her
worship and adoration. Show _____ that
"the world is fading away," but if she does your
will she will "live forever" (I John 2:17).

Today I declare that _____ will no
longer worship the things of this world. She
will be faithful to the God whose love knows
no bounds!

Day 55 Promise

"Come to me, all of you who are weary and carry heavy burdens, and I will give you rest."
–Jesus
Matthew 11:28

My Prayer

Dear Jesus, I love your gentle invitation to the weary and broken to "Come." And you offer them the gentle, compassionate promise of "rest."

I marvel at this: there are no requirements, no hoops to jump through, no puzzles to solve, no quests to win, no expensive gifts to purchase. _____ is simply invited to come into the presence of the King of Kings; and when she does, the King has a gift waiting for her. I praise Jehovah Shalom, *the God of peace!* In a chaotic and demanding world, you give your children rest.

Today I declare _____ will come to Jesus, leave her burdens at the cross, and find eternal rest!

Day 56 Promise

But as for you, _____ ... I have called you back ... so that you can serve me. For I have chosen you and will not throw you away.

Isaiah 41: 8a, 9

My Prayer

Lord, this verse reminds me that _____ is called and chosen by God. She is your treasure, not worthless trash to discard. An important kingdom job is waiting for her, and it is time for her to get to work. Let her hear your voice and heed your call!

The enemy wants her to believe she is worthless, damaged goods. I come against that lie in the name of Jesus! Lord, you see the value and good in her. Help _____ to see herself through your eyes.

Today I declare that _____ is coming back to serve the Father. Assure her that she is wanted, needed and loved!

Day 57 Promise

Without wavering, let us hold tightly to the hope we say we have, for God can be trusted to keep his promise.

Hebrews 10:23

My Prayer

Lord, I confess, sometimes I get very discouraged when I see how the enemy is using and abusing her. The ups and downs of life when one loves a prodigal can be such an emotional roller coaster! Help!

That is when I remember I have to keep my eyes on you—the PROMISE KEEPER! I know you are at work right now, fulfilling every promise. I can *completely* trust you.

Today I declare that God will keep each and every promise he has made to me. I will hold on tightly to hope because that hope is firmly anchored in Christ Jesus! This story will end well!

Day 58 Promise

...he called _____ out of the darkness into his wonderful light.

I Peter 2:9

My Prayer

In the name of Jesus, I proclaim that God is calling you, _____ ! Come out of the darkness and remember who you are!

You belong to God. You are not meant to be like the world. You are set apart as one of God's chosen.

Today I declare that when you finally step into the light and take your rightful place in God's kingdom YOU WILL SHINE! Talk about standing out in a crowd!

Into marvelous light I'm running,
Out of darkness, out of shame.
By the cross you are the truth,
You are the life, you are the way
My dead heart now is beating,
My deepest stains now clean.
Your breath fills up my lungs.
Now I'm free. Now I'm free!
Lift my hands and spin around,
See the light that I have found.
Oh the marvelous light
Marvelous light[9]

Day 59 Promise

Your children will rebuild the deserted ruins of your cities.

Isaiah 58:12a

My Prayer

Lord, I believe _____ is destined to help increase the population of heaven. That is what this family does. We are kingdom builders.

Today I declare the time has come for _____ to take her position in the family business. We never run short of customers. Everywhere we look people's lives are empty, broken and lie in ruin. Let's introduce them to Jesus, and let's do it together.

Day 60 Promise

And we know that God causes everything to work together for the good of those who love God and are called according to his purpose for them.

Romans 8:28

My Prayer

Lord, this verse gives me so much hope! *Everything* includes mistakes, intentional sin, even unbelief, yet somehow you will bring good from all of it.

WOW. WOW. WOW!!

It reminds me of the artists who take pieces of broken pottery and design a beautiful mosaic out of it. You are able to create something beautiful out of her brokenness, too.

This promise is for *those who love God and are called* for your *purpose.* I pray that _____ would fall in love with you once again and surrender to your purpose and plan.

Today I declare that God will work all things together for good for _____.

Day 61 Promise

For this son of mine was dead and has now returned to life. He was lost, but now he is found. So the party began.

Luke 15:24

My Prayer

Let the party begin! I cannot wait to say those words! One day my prodigal will return to her heavenly Father. Lord, let it be soon.

All my life, I heard so many sermons on the parable of the prodigal son. They all started to sound the same, and I would tune out or critique the speaker on his/her ability to say something I had not heard before. Oh God, forgive my smug pride! I never imagined this would be *my* story. Now, I cannot hear this passage enough! It is life to me! Thank you Jesus for this beautiful picture of the Father's love.

Today I declare _____ is found and she is alive and well! Time to throw the party of all parties!

Day 62 Promise

But angels are only servants. They are spirits sent from God to care for those who will receive salvation.

Hebrews 1:14

My Prayer

Lord, I thank you for the assurance that _____ is under the care and protection of angels. I believe you have assigned several angels to watch over her because she is marked for salvation.

Empower your mighty angelic forces to fight off demonic spirits that try to harm her. Just as you sent angels to shut the mouths of lions when Daniel was in the lions' den, I know you will keep evil predators from destroying her. Thank you for promising to protect her wherever she goes.

Today I declare that God's ministering angels are watching over _____, keeping her safe until the day of salvation.

Day 63 Promise

He is a mighty savior. He will rejoice over
_____ with great gladness ... He will
exult over _____ by singing a happy
song.

Zephaniah 3:17b

My Prayer

_____, you bring God joy! The God
of the universe rejoices over you! Get ready for
a new day of hope! No more fearing the
Father, no more shame. Your mighty Savior
has defeated death, hell and the grave. He
wants nothing more than to have relationship
with you. You are his daughter, and he
delights in you!

In Jesus name, I declare that one day
_____ will experience glad and happy
times in the presence of her marvelous
heavenly Father.

Day 64 Promise

"This promise* is to you and to your children ... all who have been called by the Lord our God ... Save yourselves from this generation that has gone astray!" -Peter

Acts 2:39,40

My Prayer

_____, the promise* waiting for you includes forgiveness, salvation and the baptism of the Holy Spirit (Acts 2:38).

Jesus, please give her the courage to leave her lost generation. She must be willing to go against the flow of culture. This will require supernatural strength and determination that only you can provide. Once she makes her move to go, I pray that she doesn't just walk; let her run to you! Holy Spirit, may she feel the urgency of making a decision for you before it is too late! Open her eyes to see just how lost all the people around her truly are—they are like the blind leading the blind. Like Lot, go quickly and don't look back! Save yourself, _____!

Today I declare that _____ will leave her old life behind to claim the promise of the Trinity: God's forgiveness, salvation in Jesus, and Holy Ghost power.

Day 65 Promise

But the Lord still waits for you, _____, to come to him so he can show you his love and compassion.

Isaiah 30:18

My Prayer

Lord, you long for _____ to come to you. You stand ready to heap compassion, grace and love upon her. I know that day is coming!

Jesus, your patience with her amazes me, and I am forever grateful. I struggle in that area (understatement!). Waiting is so hard for me— agonizing at times! Is it possible to make this salvation process speed up?! Thank you for being patient with my impatience. Help me remember that you are not being slow in keeping your promise, you are giving her more time to repent (2 Peter. 3:9). What a wonderful Savior!

At the appointed time, I declare that _____ will willingly run into the everlasting, loving arms of her Father.

Day 66 Promise

"And I, the Son of Man, have come to seek and
save those like him who are lost." – Jesus

Luke 19:10

My Prayer

You came to seek out and save the lost.
Thank you for pursuing _____, Lord.

Jesus, when you said "like him" you
were referring to Zacchaeus, a "notorious
sinner" (Luke 19:7). Many people didn't think
he was worthy of salvation, but you proved
them wrong! You came for people just like
him! I thank you for the instant
transformation you made in Zacchaeus's life.
He went from thief and swindler to generous
giver. You have the power to transform lives,
because you make all things new!

Today I declare the Son of Man will find
and save _____. Just like Zacchaeus, her
conversion will result in dramatic change that
no one can deny!

Day 67 Promise

"Didn't I tell you that you will see God's glory if you believe?" – Jesus

John 11:40

My Prayer

Hallelujah! You are the God who can raise the dead! Jesus, just as you asked this question to Martha outside the tomb of Lazarus, you ask me the same question now. In many ways, my prodigal is like a dead person. When you call her forth, she will be wrapped in some foul-smelling grave clothes that will need changing. But first things first ... Jesus, I ask you to speak life into her right now. I know she can be free from her tomb of death. Lord, I want to see your glory all over _____! I believe!

Today I believe and declare that many will see God's glory when God raises _____ from death to life!

Day 68 Promise

Teach your children to choose the right path, and when they are older, they will remain upon it.

Proverbs 22:6

My Prayer

Lord, you know I did my best to raise _____ according to your word. Sometimes the enemy attempts to lay guilt and blame on me for things I did and things I failed to do. Please silence the mouth of the accuser who mockingly sneers, *this is all your fault.*

I believe I was a good Christian example to her, but I am certainly not perfect. Forgive me for any mistakes I made that might have turned her against you. Jesus, thank you for mercy; help me receive your forgiveness and your grace.

Today I declare this prophetic guarantee: I taught _____ God's way, so one day she will choose your path and stay on it.

Day 69 Promise

"Those who search for me will surely find me."
                                    —Wisdom
                              Proverbs 8:17

My Prayer

Lord, my beloved is searching for something to fill her spiritual void. Right now she is trying to find a "truth" that can top what she already knows. Please protect _____ from being enticed and entrapped by a false religion or belief system. Lord, show her ALL truth is God's truth. Truth is a person: Jesus!

Jesus, one of the saddest stories in the Bible is when Pilot stood before you and asked, "What is truth?" Then, he immediately walked away, never waiting for an answer. Pilot was staring into the eyes of TRUTH and he missed it! I pray that when _____ comes face to face with you, she will SEE you for who you are: the God of grace and truth!

Today I declare that when her search is over, _____ will find herself in the presence of Jesus, enjoying wisdom, life and the favor of the Lord (Prov. 9:35).

Day 70 Promise

... He is able to accomplish infinitely more
than we would ever dare to ask or hope.

Ephesians 3:20

My Prayer

Jesus, I am asking for BIG things for
_____! I ask that you give her a
revelation of Jesus, salvation, freedom, and
unshakeable faith. Bless her with vision,
talents, gifts, abilities, and a willingness to
use them to serve others. Add to these a
kingdom mindset, Christian friends, the right
job, a love for truth, a love for your word, a
tender heart, etc. That "etc." means I believe
you can do infinitely MORE, too! Hallelujah!
Today I declare my God is able to
accomplish MIND-BLOWING miracles for
_____. In every area of her life, may God
be glorified!

Day 71 Promise

I will put a desire in _____'s heart to worship me, and _____ will never leave me.

Jeremiah 32:40

My Prayer

God, only you are able to change a woman's inner longings and desires. I praise you Jehovah Mekadesh; you are *the Lord who sanctifies.* You told the Israelites to set themselves apart from the world, and you would make them holy (Leviticus 20: 7,8).

I pray _____ sets herself apart from the world and trusts you to do the rest. May she grow to become more and more like you each day, simultaneously growing in her passion to praise you! I thank you for putting a heart of worship in _____.

Today I declare that _____ is a true worshipper and a faithful follower of Jesus!

Day 72 Promise

He will turn the hearts of the fathers to their children, and the hearts of the children to their fathers.

Malachi 4:6

My Prayer

Father God, I ask you to turn _____'s heart toward you. Malachi prophesied that Elijah's preaching would cause the children's hearts to return to their parents. Four hundred years later, John's preaching would turn men's hearts toward Jesus. Now, in these last days, I pray you send _____ a prophetic message that would reignite her love for Jesus. Open the eyes of her heart!

Today I declare that _____ will hear a prophetic word from God that turns her heart back to her Heavenly Father!

Day 73 Promise

But this is what the Lord says … "I will fight those who fight you, and I will save your children."

Isaiah 49:25

My Prayer

It's on now! Those are fighting words! My loving ally, El Shaddai, *the Almighty God*, is going after _____. Lord, you know she has been taken captive by the enemy. I pray you retrieve and release her. When you do, will you annihilate the demonic terrorist forces that stole her from me? Crush the tyrannical tyrants beneath your feet and curse them from ever harming another again!

Today I declare that God is fighting for _____ and he will save her from captivity!

Day 74 Promise

"I will come and heal *her*." – Jesus

Matthew 8:7

My Prayer

Dear Jesus, just as the Roman officer responded to this promise with, "Just say the word...," I also believe one word from you is all it will take. When you saw the centurion's faith, you were "amazed" (Matt. 8:10). I want to have that same kind of faith! Say the word over _____, Lord. Heal her heart, soul, and mind.

Come and dwell in her. Make her heart your home. Renew her mind. I praise you Jehovah-Rapha, you are the *God who heals!*

Today I declare that Jesus will heal

_____.

Faith sees the invisible, believes the unbelievable, and receives the impossible. [10]
Corrie Ten Boom

Day 75 Promise

For _____ is God's masterpiece. He has created *her* anew in Christ Jesus, so that _____ can do the good things he planned for *her* long ago.

Ephesians 2:10

My Prayer

Jesus, before the foundations of the world you planned *good things* for _____ to do. The enemy greedily desired God's masterpiece for himself. He used trickery and deceit to steal my loved one away. Jesus, please find my treasure and return her to her rightful home. I believe everything that has happened in her life so far, the good and the bad, is moving her toward your greater purpose.

_____, I speak to the woman of faith inside you and say, "Wake up and believe once again! Jesus has the power to make you brand new!"

Today I declare _____ is the Creator's masterpiece! A work of art so magnificent that when people see her doing God's work they will be amazed!

Day 76 Promise

"… But take heart, because I have overcome the world." – Jesus

John 16:33

My Prayer

Dear Jesus, sometimes it seems like my prodigal has been swallowed up by the world. The enticements, the temptations, the pleasures—and all the regrets, sorrows, and consequences that accompany them.

Then I remember this promise and my heart sings! Satan's agenda to control this world was defeated long ago when my Savior went to the cross. Jesus is forever crowned Champion of the World, Master of the Universe, King of Kings and Lord of Lords!

Today I declare that the world can no longer devour my beloved, because Jesus has overcome the world!

Day 77 Promise

Your faithfulness extends to every generation, as enduring as the earth you created.

Psalm 119:90

My Prayer

Dear God, please bless the generations that come through _____, whether physical children or spiritual children, or both. Our family is committed to praising your great faithfulness from generation to generation.

Today I declare that _____ will continue the legacy of faith in our family.

I have a dream for you
It's better than where you've been
It's bigger than your imagination
You're gonna find real love
And you're gonna hold your kids
You'll change the course of generations
'Cause you're my child
You're my chosen, You are loved
And I will restore all that was broken
You are loved
And just like the seasons change
Winter into spring
You're bringing new life to your family tree now
Yes you are [11]

Day 78 Promise

I will make the darkness bright before
_____ and smooth out the road ahead of
her... I will not forsake *her*.

Isaiah 42:16b

My Prayer

How great is your love, oh God! My
prodigal is blindly walking along a dark,
unfamiliar path. Yet, you promise to go before
her, clearing the way and shining a spotlight
so she can see. Best of all, she is not alone! I
worship you my merciful and gracious God!

Today I declare God's promise to stay
with and help _____ while she walks this
perilous path. I know you will lead her to
safety!

Day 79 Promise

_____, you must remain faithful to what you have been taught from the beginning. If you do, you will continue to live in fellowship with the Son and with the Father.

I John 2: 24

My Prayer

Lord, once again remind _____ of all the scriptures, Bible stories, and real life faith experiences from her past ... all precious memories. They are like seeds planted deep within her. Over the years, those seeds were watered and fertilized. I speak to those seeds in her—in Jesus name, burst forth and grow! I believe it is harvest time!

Stir in her a desire to be in communion with you once again. How cold and alone she must feel, living outside of your fellowship. It must be like hell on earth. Let your love be the magnet that draws her back into the Father's arms and into the light of the Son.

Today I declare that _____ will live in fellowship with Father and Son, staying faithful to your word.

Day 80 Promise

Let _____ turn to the Lord that he may
have mercy on *her*. Yes, turn to our God, for he
will abundantly pardon.

Isaiah 55:7

My Prayer

Turn. Mercy waits for you, _____.
Complete, total freedom is yours. Surrender to
the one who loves you.

When I picture what it looks like to
"abundantly pardon," I can't help but see the
Father in the prodigal son story. His son had
squandered half of his inheritance and left
home in dishonor. Nevertheless, as soon as the
Father sees the son coming, he RUNS to him!
Then he orders the servants to prepare the
fattened calf. Next, he showers affection on
him, wraps him in an expensive robe and puts
a costly ring on his finger. His son was not just
forgiven, he was fully restored to a place of
honor in the family!

Today I declare _____ will turn to
Jesus! Father God, I praise you for the over-
the-top gifts of love you are preparing for my
prodigal!

Day 81 Promise

For I am about to do a brand-new thing ... I
will make a pathway in the wilderness for
_____ to come home.

Isaiah 43:19

My Prayer

Dear Lord, _____ needs her own
exodus experience. So many times in history
your people found themselves ensnared in
slavery. Each time, the people would cry out to
God, and you would save them! I believe you
are about to free my beloved and lead her out
of bondage to a place of belonging. I believe
she is already on the path home.

Today I declare a brand new start for
_____. Regardless of how wild her
wilderness is, you are making a clear path
that will lead her home!

*It is always hard to see the purpose in wilderness
wanderings until after they are over.*[12]
John Bunyan

Day 82 Promise

The Lord Almighty will hover over
_____ as a bird hovers around its nest.
He will defend and save _____.

Isaiah 31:5a

My Prayer

Lord, you know how vulnerable my prodigal is. Thank you for this promise to hover over, protect, and rescue _____ from predators!

It is a fearsome thing to observe a mama bird watching over and defending her nest. She stays on high alert, eyes darting to and fro, chirping loudly, flapping and spreading her wings, ready to attack any intruder—another bird would have to be CRAZY to mess with her!

Lord, your ability to protect and defend your children is like that, *times infinity*! Jesus, the devil is trying to snatch our little bird from the nest. I pray you destroy the works of the enemy once-and-for-all, never to harm another innocent life.

Today I declare the Lord Almighty hovers over _____ to protect and save her!

Day 83 Promise

Yes, what joy for those whose record the Lord has cleared of sin, whose lives are lived in complete honesty!

Psalm 32:2

My Prayer

Joy is coming for _____!

Thank you for including David's story in your word, Lord. David's lust-fueled sin against Bathsheba and his diabolical plot to murder Uriah show that even an anointed king of Israel is capable of doing downright despicable things! Still, the moment he confessed his sins to you, all guilt was wiped away, leaving him shouting for joy!

As long as David tried to hide his sins "your hand of discipline was heavy" on him and he was "miserable" (v. 3-4). Lord, I pray you would make my prodigal sick and tired of living with unconfessed sin. Let her feel the weight of rebellion lift off her as she confesses her hidden sins to you. From this day on, let her be known as a woman of integrity.

Today I declare that _____ will live an honest, joy-filled life! The Lord will clear her of sin, remove all traces of guilt, and cause her to shout for joy!

Day 84 Promise

Take delight in the Lord, and he will give you your heart's desire.

Psalm 37:4

My Prayer

Lord, this promise is for me. You know my heart's desire is to see _____ serving and loving you. Even if this was the only promise I had for my beloved, this one says it all. Jesus, you are the joy of my life, my greatest delight, and my reason for living. I know her faith story will end well because you ALWAYS keep your promises.

Today I declare that God will give me my heart's desire! _____ will come home to Jesus.

Day 85 Promise

If two of you agree down here on earth
concerning anything you ask, my Father in
heaven will do it for you.

Matthew 18:19

My Prayer

Praise the Lord! This promise is a slam
dunk for me! You only ask that two people join
in agreement. I thank you for the friends and
family who have already joined me in praying
for my beloved. Lord, I ask that you send me
even more prayer partners; let there be round-
the-clock prayers going up for _____.
Father in heaven, I thank you for fulfilling
your promise to save and free my prodigal!

Today I declare the promise of praying
in agreement over _____. Two by two we
are bombarding heaven for her salvation and
freedom. Father, I know you will do it!

Day 86 Promise

Long ago, even before he made the world, God loved _____ and chose _____ in Christ to be holy.

Ephesians 1:4a

My Prayer

Lord, _____ belongs to your dearly loved Son. She was chosen long ago to live in Christ. It is hard to fathom just how long you have loved her. Your plan to be in relationship with her is unchanging, no matter how far or how long she runs from you. You save us, not because we deserve it, but because we are part of your greater plan. Let _____ accept the fact that she is a chosen daughter of God, adopted into the family. Let her embrace this high calling!

Today I declare that _____ is loved by God and chosen to be holy in Christ!

Day 87 Promise

I can never escape from your Spirit! I can
never get away from your presence!

Psalm 139:7

My Prayer

Lord, I am undone by this realization.
You are a holy and righteous God, yet you
choose to live amongst mere mortals. When I
imagine some of the sordid places my prodigal
goes into, it blows my mind that your presence
goes in, too. I remember how the prodigal
came to himself when he was eating with the
pigs. That means your spirit was with him in
the filthy, foul-smelling pigpen, drawing him
back to the Father. Oh gracious God, thank
you for the life-changing power of the presence
of the Holy Spirit! I know you are with
_____ right now, bringing her to her
senses and wooing her back to Jesus.

Today I declare the Holy Spirit will
never leave _____. Make her aware of
your presence!

Day 88 Promise

He led _____ from the darkness
and deepest gloom; he snapped *her*
chains.   Psalm 107:14

My Prayer

Jesus, my prodigal is in such a dark
place, she cannot see how to get out; and even
if she tried to leave, she is chained up with no
way to break loose.

I thank you for this verse, because just
as you rescued the exiled Israelites imprisoned
in Babylon, you will rescue my beloved, too.
During that time, many of the rebellious Jews
ended up miserable prisoners in chains,
broken by hard labor. In their distress, they
finally cried out for help. Immediately, you
"broke their prison gates of bronze" and "cut
apart their bars of iron" (Ps. 107:16). You
came just in time. They were wretched and
wasting away, and you saved them from
certain death.

Today I declare that Jesus is the
CHAIN BREAKER! He is leading _____
from her dark dungeon of death and breaking
every chain!

Day 89 Promise

Listen to me! You can pray for anything, and if you believe, you will have it.

Mark 11:24

My Prayer

Dear Jesus, I am listening! You are encouraging me to pray in faith, so I will. I know some conditions must be met before I do. First, I must believe in YOU, and I do! Second, I must not have unforgiveness in my heart, so if there is any, please show me (Mark 11:25). I do not want anything to keep you from hearing my request. Finally, my prayer must align with your will. I know it does, because you came to seek and to save the lost.

I ask that you save _____ and fulfill your purpose in her life.

Today I declare _____ will be saved, because I believe in a miracle-working God who can do anything!

Day 90 Promise

... won't God, who gave us Christ, also give us everything else?

Romans 8:32

My Prayer

Thank you, Father God, that nothing can separate us from your love. You love my prodigal so much. Even while knowing she would deny you and live outside your laws, you still gave _____ the ultimate gift— you sent Jesus. How could I think *for one second* that you will not do EVERYTHING in your power to save my beloved?

Today I declare that my God, because of his generous and reckless love, will bring _____ back to Jesus. She is born again.

Day 91 Promise

But if you give up your life for my sake and for the sake of the Good News, you will find true life.

Mark 8:35b

My Prayer

Lord, in order to follow you, we must willingly lay some things down and pick up our cross—a life of self-denial and surrender to God's will. You require nothing less than ultimate submission from your followers.

_____ knows this. She once thought she could follow you and still practice sin, but she knows better now. Let her realize that all her worldly pleasures are temporary, hollow and empty. Only in complete surrender to you will she find abundant, eternal life.

Today I declare that _____ will choose to give up everything to serve Jesus. True life begins now!

Bear your cross as you wait for the crown
Tell the world of the treasure you found [13]

Day 92 Promise

As far as I am concerned, God turned into good what you meant for evil.

Genesis 50:20

My Prayer

Good Father, this one verse captures the very essence of the entire gospel. We are all a bunch of mess-ups and misfits, duped and deceived by the devil; but because of your extravagant grace everything gets turned upside down. New for old, joy for sorrow, light for darkness, strength for weakness—the list goes on and on. God, you really are good *all* the time.

The enemy has thrown everything in his playbook at my prodigal, but he will not win! In the end, God will be glorified and the kingdom will advance! Good things are coming! Praise the Lord!

Today I declare that everything the enemy meant for evil, God will turn into something good for _____ !

Day 93 Promise

The wicked perish and are gone, but the children of the godly stand firm.

Proverbs 12:7

My Prayer

Lord, I believe one day _____ will stand for righteousness. She will not bow to popular opinion or cultural norms, but she will live her life according to your word. She will not be like the foolish man who built his house on sand, but she will build her house on the rock of Jesus Christ. When the storms of life come, she will not get swept away and perish.

Lord, standing for truth in this world requires boldness and courage, so I pray you fill _____ with your Holy Spirit power. Teach her to put the armor of God on each day. Give her a love for your word, so she can use the sword of the spirit to defeat the works of the enemy.

Today I declare this promise over _____: she is part of a godly family and she will stand firm!

Day 94 Promise

I will search for my lost ones who strayed away, and I will bring them safely home again.

Ezekiel 34:16a

My Prayer

Jehovah Rohi, *the Lord is my Shepherd*, I call on your name. Once again, I ask you to search for my lost prodigal. I thank you, good Shepherd, for always putting the needs of your flock first. When one goes missing, however, you do something that may seem irresponsible: you leave the ninety-nine to go after the one. How passionate you are for lost souls! Praise Jehovah Rohi!

Gentle Shepherd, when you find the lost sheep, you don't punish it. Instead, you bind up its wounds and carry it to safety. Thank you for being gentle with my beloved, too. Your great compassion and mercy is too much for my mind to comprehend.

Today I declare Jehovah Rohi is searching for _____ and bringing her safely home!

Day 95 Promise

"Your children will come back to you from the distant land of the enemy. There is hope for your future," says the Lord. "Your children will come again to their own land."

Jeremiah 31:16b-17

My Prayer

Dear Lord, she feels so distant from me. We used to be so close. We had so much to say to each other. Now, our conversations seem shallow because so many subjects are off limits. It comforts me to know you understand how I feel. You have had rebellious children too...

You walked and talked every evening with Adam and Eve, gave them everything they could ever desire, yet they disobeyed and betrayed you. If you, the perfect Father, could be rejected by your children, then it could happen to any of us.

Lord, thank you for this vivid promise that summarizes our future so clearly. Today I declare that _____ will leave the land of the enemy and come back to her own land, a land of love and hope.

Day 96 Promise

They will see in our history the faithful love of
the Lord.

Psalm 107:43b

My Prayer

Lord, there have been moments when I
wonder what people say about our family. Do
they look at our prodigal and blame us for her
choices? Do they talk about us, judge us,
gossip about us, etc. Oh God, help me, in those
moments, to take every thought captive and
make it bow to the authority of Jesus Christ.
Those kinds of thoughts are from the enemy,
and *they must go in the name of Jesus!*

Your word promises me that in the end,
people will see God's faithful love in our
family. If we are remembered at all, let people
say that God's goodness and mercy was
evident in all of our lives. Most importantly,
let each of our names be recorded in the
Lamb's Book of Life!

Today I declare that when people look
at our family, especially _____, they will
see the faithful love of the Lord!

Day 97 Promise

And this is the will of God, that I should not lose even one of all those he has given me, but that I should raise them to eternal life at the last day.

John 6:39

My Prayer

Thank you Jesus! You made it so clear that it IS God's will for _____ to be saved and have eternal life! And it is NOT God's will for her to be lost.

Wherever she is, I pray she would hunger and thirst for you, Jesus. You are the bread of life and the living water. Only you can satisfy.

Jesus, you taught your disciples to pray "Thy kingdom come, thy will be done" (Matt. 6:10). Right now I speak that prayer over my prodigal. I pray *your will be done*, that you would save her and grant her eternal life.

Today, I declare God's will—salvation and eternal life—for _____!

Day 98 Promise

"I will be found by _____," says the Lord.
Jeremiah 29:14a

My Prayer

YES & AMEN! Her search will lead her straight to you, Jesus! Please give her that "Aha!" moment soon, Lord. That awareness that everything she has been looking for has been there the whole time.

Today I declare that _____ will find her way back to you!

To fall in love with God is the greatest romance; to seek him the greatest adventure; to find him, the greatest human achievement.[14] St. Augustine

Day 99 Promise

You will show _____ the way of life,
granting _____ the joy of your presence
and the pleasures of living with you forever.

Psalm 16:11

My Prayer

Heavenly Father, the pleasures you offer are not temporary, they are eternal. Show her all she is missing. Unimaginable opportunities and grand adventures await! She focuses on what she will lose; give her a vision of what she will gain. The benefits of living in companionship with you, the source of real joy! The pleasure of living in your presence, the giver of life and peace!

Today I declare this beautiful promise: God will show _____ the way to a life filled with joy and pleasure forevermore!

Day 100 Promise

And now I entrust you, _____, to God and the word of his grace—His message that is able to build you up and give you an inheritance with all those he has set apart for himself.

Acts 20:32

My Prayer

Father God, I give _____ to you. I can trust you with her faith. She belongs to you and always has. She is set apart, called and chosen by you.

Holy Spirit, I know you are working behind the scenes to work out every detail of my beloved's homecoming. I thank you for your relentless pursuit of my prodigal.

Jesus, I know the instant you reveal yourself to her, she will be undone. She will fall madly in love with you for the rest of her life. You already paid her ransom in full with your precious blood. Now, I ask that you go get her and bring her home.

Today, I declare all the Lord's promises are true for _____, because all of them are backed by the honor of his GREAT name (Ps. 138:2b, 18:30).

Dear Prodigal Prayer Warrior,

If you prayed through ALL one hundred promises in this book, please let me be the first to say, "WELL DONE."

Maybe nothing has changed (that you can see), and you find yourself a bit discouraged. I know the feeling. Praying for a lost loved one takes commitment and emotional fortitude, so you might discover that you need to take a few days to breathe and change your focus. I encourage you to spend time just worshipping God, giving thanks for all the good things happening in your life right now. My prayer for you is that after some down time, you start praying these promises again. A breakthrough is coming, and your prayers matter. Don't give up! God always keeps his promises!

Maybe your experience is exactly the opposite. Your prayers have been answered, and your prodigal has found her way back to Jesus! Yay God!! I celebrate with you, and I would LOVE to hear your story! Please email me at **promisesforprodigals@gmail.com** and tell me all about it. May God empower you with grace and shine his favor on you and yours!

Blessings,
Lori

NOTES

1 Cory Asbury, Caleb Culver, and Ran Jackson. "Reckless Love." *Reckless Love,* Bethel Music, 2017.

2 Scott Wesley Brown, "He Will Carry You." *Sparrow Double Play,* Universal Music Publishing Group, Capitol Christian Music Group, 1982.

3 *Smith Wigglesworth (2006). Smith Wigglesworth on Prayer, p.78, Destiny Image Publishers.*

4 Facebook post by Billy Graham from Aug 04, 2012.

5 Don Moen, "The Mercy Seat." *The Mercy Seat with Don Moen*, Integrity Publishing, 2000.

6 Mark Batterson. http://ohamanda.com/2013/01/17/5-tips-on-prayerful-parenting-from-mark-batterson/

7 Anonymous. "I Have Decided to Follow Jesus."

8 E.E. Hewitt, "When We All Get to Heaven." 1898.

9) Charlie Hall and Steve J. Hindalong. "Marvelous Light." *Live Roots*, Universal Music Publishing Group, 2004.

10 *Corrie Ten Boom (1985). Jesus is Victor, Fleming H Revell Company.*

11 Jason Houser, Jason C. Houser, Matthew West, and Matthew Joseph West, "Family Tree." *The Story of Your Life*, Warner/Chappell Music, Inc, Amplified Administration, 2010.

12 John Bunyan, *The Pilgrim's Progress: From This World to That Which Is to Come.*

13 Mack Brock, Chris Brown, Steven Furtick, and Wade Joye. "O Come to the Altar." *Elevation Worship Here As In Heaven*, Elevation Worship Publishing, 2015.

14 Saint Augustine. https://relevantmagazine.com/god/15-augustine-quotes-helped-shape-modern-christian-thought

Eric Kennedy
Addres marriage Book Podcast

Made in the USA
Columbia, SC
21 December 2023